AMUSING CONFESSIONS OF AN INTERNATIONAL CONSULTANT

Mark C Hehl

Copyright © 2017 by Mark C Hehl

All rights reserved. No part of this book may be used or reproduced in any manner without written permission from the author, except in the case of brief quotations embodied in critical articles or reviews. mhehl@charter.net

Cover design by Hicham Boughdadi: Hicham@webzwin.com

This is dedicated to my best friend and wife, Olga, who supported me taking the plunge into independent consulting and who tolerated my being away from home so often.

CONTENTS
ACKNOWLEDGEMENTS
PREFACE
PART I "IT IS NOT RIGHT OR WRONG, GOOD OR BAD, IT IS JUST DIFFERENT"
CHAPTER 1: NOT ENGAGING THE CULTURE = COMPANY FAILURE
CHAPTER 2: "I TOLD YOU VERY CLEARLY" A COMMUNICATION MESS
CHAPTER 3: PROTECTING A BAD DESIGN
CHAPTER 4: AN UPRISING ON A FERRY
CHAPTER 5: HABLA CON EL JEFE (SPEAK WITH THE BOSS)
CHAPTER 6: THE BLACKOUT
CHAPTER 7: NO CHRISTMAS DELIVERIES, A $5 MILLION LOSS
CHAPTER 8: ONE-CHILD POLICY
CHAPTER 9: DOING IT FOR THE WRONG REASON
PART II   ON THE LIGHTER SIDE - AMUSING EXPERIENCES
CHAPTER 10: "...BUT I DO NOT KNOW HOW TO DRIVE"
CHAPTER 11: DO NOT PLAY GAMES WITH INTERPRETATION
CHAPTER 12: EATING BREAKFAST WITH ADAM SANDLER
CHAPTER 13: NO SCRAMBLED EGGS FOR ME
CHAPTER 14: DO FIRE EXTINGUISHERS REALLY NEED TO WORK?
CHAPTER 15: LEFT-HANDED CHOPSTICKS
CHAPTER 16: SOUP ON A PLANE
CHAPTER 17: THESE STAIRS ARE A CHALLENGE
CHAPTER 18: WHY DOES HE CARE?
PART III   INTERESTING FACILITIES - TO SAY THE LEAST
CHAPTER 19: THE FIRE
CHAPTER 20: THE EMPLOYEES WERE EATING LUNCH ON THE FLOOR
CHAPTER 21: PAYING TO MAKE A BAD SITUATION WORSE
CHAPTER 22: EVERYTHING IS REWORKED
CHAPTER 23: ARE SUPPLIERS THE ENEMY?
CHAPTER 24: MY WORST EXPERIENCE
CHAPTER 25: THERE WERE MANY POSITIVE OUTCOMES
CHAPTER 26: CONCLUSION

Acknowledgements

There are many individuals to thank for their assistance and support in bringing this book to life; more than I can mention here.

First and foremost, my sincere gratitude goes to Louis Traverson, who inspired me to undertake this project now rather than after retirement. I do not plan to retire and without him this book would, most likely, never exist.

To my editor-in-chief, Olga, I thank her for her tireless hours editing the manuscript, correcting and improving my grammar. Her eagle eyes and keen attention to detail helped to make the text more readable.

I asked my good friend, Eduardo Santana, to consider writing a praise for this book. He not only did that but went the extra mile and provided me with many valuable suggestions, which enhanced it.

My thanks go to Marvin White of BizProfitPro, LLC. and Christel Pellerin of PROJECT ALA CARTE, Inc. for their kind words of praise.

There are two young women that I have had the joy of seeing grow into accomplished professional adults. My thanks go to Anna Lepeley, PhD and Lauren Sequenzia, MBA for their technical assistance. In the past, I used to advise and coach them, now they have become my coaches.

My consulting career would not be the same if it weren't for The DESARA Group, Inc. I thank Dave Sanicola and Karen Rawson for taking me on and believing in me when the company was formed. I have had the opportunity to work with fantastic consultants at DESARA.

I thank all my clients who put complete trust in my ability to not only improve their organizations but provide an opportunity for their further growth and development. My true passion is developing individuals and organizations. Consulting allowed me to live my dreams.

Mark Hehl
Woodbury, CT, USA
October 2017

Preface

The world is getting smaller, especially when it comes to the world of business. The amount of international trade grows daily, this increases the need for consultants who can handle themselves in an ever-changing arena.

This book is the result of twenty-four years of assisting many organizations in over forty countries covering multiple industries / technologies. Most of my projects involved technology transfer or operational excellence. I also had the privilege to speak at numerous professional society events held at various world locations. These presentation topics were related to conflict resolution, project management, operational excellence and cultural issues.

During my travels and extended stays in five continents, I encountered a variety of amusing experiences, cross-cultural *faux pas* and was exposed to many production facilities (too many to count). Most of them were well managed and the projects that I ran were fruitful, resulting in quality improvement, cost reduction and successful product releases. I have experienced great management throughout the world and, in a few cases the other extreme, terrible execution resulting in disaster. Over these years, I have seen a gradual operational improvement in third world businesses and I expect this improvement to continue. There are excellent and poor organizations in every country. I have heard remarks that all production facilities in X country are bad. This is simply incorrect.

My initial intent was to just amuse the reader with some interesting experiences. While writing, I saw the need to also educate the reader on the importance of cultural savvy when interacting with foreigners. This prompted me to add a section on cultural mistakes. Upon completion of these two sections I began to describe some dysfunctional situations that I was involved with in various parts of the world (even in the USA). This book then slowly evolved into something that would be educational.

Being an engineer, my writing style is consistent with a technical professional and sometimes dull. Hopefully, my attempts to overcome this were beneficial. I attempted to write in interesting layman's terms especially in Part III. I trust that readers with and without a background in technology and operations will find this useful.

To protect both the innocent, guilty and the organizations that I represented, I did not identify the organization and in some cases the country. My clients put their trust in me and I would never betray that trust.

Hopefully, some of these lessons will prove useful to the reader performing this line of work.

Part I

It is not right or wrong, good or bad, it is just different" *

* This quote was a response from the writer after a trip to Asia. I was telling a family member about something experienced while there. She responded with a negative remark (I cannot remember exactly what it was). The above was my response. The point here is that one will encounter different behaviors and communication methods while traveling abroad. It is wise to not judge these differences, just accept them. Also, what we do and accept as normal will very often seem strange to foreigners.

1. Not engaging the culture = company failure

How an international organization blew it.

While working as a consultant for a European organization that had operations in Europe, North America and in various Asian countries, I witnessed firsthand the importance of applying cultural savviness and what happens when an organization does not.

One of their divisions located in an Asian country (not China) was buying product kits from suppliers in China. The final product was then assembled in this Asian country and sold domestically. Performing the final assembly in-country allowed them to avoid some import duties. I was engaged to resolve the numerous quality issues that were being experienced. Most of my time on that engagement was spent in my client's office in China. While trying to improve the situation, I found myself adjudicating many conflicts between the division buying the kits and the suppliers. There was constant conflict and I needed to make frequent trips back and forth to resolve these disagreements. The two countries had vastly different cultures and I soon realized that this was a major cause of the problems.

Being that most of my time was spent in China, I coached and trained the Chinese employees on this other culture. This helped a bit, however I was redeployed by my client to another project before I had the opportunity move forward with my plan to teach the Chinese culture to the individuals in the other country. This would have helped to improve things.

While there, a recession hit and material prices dropped. I was asked to renegotiate the kit prices. I went armed with piles of supporting data on multiple visits to the suppliers in China. Each time the result was the same, absolute refusal to lower their prices. I finally developed enough of a relationship (the Mandarin word for this is *guanxi*) with one major supplier and received the reason for the refusal. They admitted that their material costs dropped but refused to lower their price because of the *grief* that my client gave them. This supplier mentioned that they expected a downturn in business and that my client was not their biggest customer but still of a significant size. It only was worth it to them to do business at the inflated price because of the problems (grief) caused by my client. My client was forced to continue to pay too much. The root cause of most the issues between the two organizations was cultural in nature.

This division could not survive this and my client sold this division at a loss.

Cross cultural training is vital for success on the world stage. Training is well worth the small cost.

2. "I told you very clearly", a communication mess

As I learned over my numerous trips overseas, cross cultural communication can screw things up when not approached correctly.

This engagement with an international client demonstrated what happens when cultural considerations are not applied during communications.

While working at a facility in China, I found myself in the middle of communication controversies, which resulted in an erosion of relationships and operational difficulties. Another division of my client, located in an English-speaking country in Asia, was having difficulty getting responses from the Chinese group that I was managing and from the suppliers. I am convinced that the underlying problem was not what was communicated, but how it was communicated.

This Chinese division supplied components to the other Asian division. The communications that were constantly coming into the Chinese organization were almost all emails. Very few phone calls were made (big error). The emails were curt, crude and demanding. Many of these emails went unanswered. I received multiple complaints from the senders indicating that the Chinese were not responding to their emails. Those sending the emails had no clue as to the reason why they were not receiving responses.

Frustration and sometimes anger ensued, almost exclusively from the Asian, English speaking, country directed at the Chinese. I found myself in the middle of this ongoing battle. My client asked me to intervene and resolve the issue, as it was impeding progress in an already very shaky and unprofitable business venture.

Here are some things that were not being approached correctly:

> The individuals on both sides did not attempt to learn about the business culture of the other side and did not apply the necessary cultural savvy. They were operating as if they were doing business within their country / culture, a common mistake that I have seen over the years as a consultant in most parts of the world.

> The native English speakers did not take into consideration that the Chinese had poor English proficiency and may not have always comprehended the emails. Generally, there is reluctance by the Chinese to admit this and ask for clarification, a face-saving issue!

> Preliminary and follow-up phone calls were not made to verify understanding and action to be taken.

> The English speakers did not realize a very important item relative to the Chinese culture. To save face (mianzi), the Chinese tend to be silent.

The lack of an email response is a response. It means that there is a problem and the other party does not want to admit it. An immediate phone call was in order at this point; however, more nasty emails kept coming.

Rather than provide an answer that is not what they think is expected by or acceptable to the other party, the Chinese will sometimes not respond at all. This does not mean "I do not care". It means that there is a problem and the sender should investigate further.

The Chinese will typically not say no or even respond when they cannot provide the information that they think will be acceptable. A yes answer can mean as little as "yes, I hear you" and nothing more. Most of the time it does not mean agreement or that action will ensue. A no answer is considered hostile and can cause either one to lose face, therefore it is not used much in areas where the Chinese culture prevails. When a Chinese person does not answer an email, it does not mean that they are ignoring the request. It sometimes means that there is a problem and the recipient is trying to save face. This response should have prompted a very tactful phone call to gather the facts and compensate for any lack of understanding. The Chinese will not typically admit that they do not understand, saving face again. An online video call is even better as one can then read others nonverbally. This allows for one to read facial clues and other non-verbal clues.

I was constantly copied on emails indicating "I told you very clearly" which irritated me. One day this statement caused me to lose it. I then called the person in charge of the group and made my disapproval known. Just because it is clear to the writer does not mean that it is clear to the recipient. I asked if the author is writing for himself / herself or for the other person who may not be proficient in English. I reminded him again: *just because it is clear to the writer does not mean that it is clear to the recipient.*

Things did improve slightly through my efforts, however cross- cultural training for both sides would have been in order. This client never allowed me to conduct any cultural training sessions, which would have helped.

Cross cultural training is a wise investment.

I sometimes beg my clients to make this investment.

3. Protecting a bad design, notwithstanding the fact that it did not work well.

Here is an example of how strong culture can be, causing a product launch disaster, lost money and a competent professional to lose his job.

While working at a client's design and development facility in the Far East (not China, but of a Chinese culture), I was involved in a situation, which taught me a valuable cultural lesson.

A design for a new product was finalized, went into production and the product was shipped to the USA. One of the many issues that I noticed was that there was no design specification, thus the designers were free to design almost anything they wanted to (not a good idea). There was no expectation of how or what this product was supposed to do and in what temperature environment it was to operate in. I was involved with the design testing and noticed that this device would shut down at high temperatures. The design team indicated that they were unable to improve the design and that this would not be much of a problem. The consumer would just have to wait for the device to cool and then continue to use it. This was not acceptable to me as this product was intended to be used outdoors. I brought this to the attention of my client contact in Europe, indicating that there would be field problems during the summer in hot regions like the southwest USA. It sometimes can get up to 120 degrees F / 49 degrees C in this area. There was an urgency to get this product to market and my recommendation to not release it to market was not taken. When projecting a performance problem, I always want to be wrong when predicting a problem, but unfortunately, I was right this time. As soon as summer hit, the product began to shut down in the southwest USA and complaints came in. Future orders were cancelled. The electronic controlling device for the motor would shut itself down when hot. Consumers were complaining: they expected that this product would perform when the outside temperature was high. The Far East design team was again unable to improve the design so that it would work at elevated temperatures.

My client panicked and a European design organization was then contracted to redesign this controller for the motor. The Far East team was then directed to send samples and the associated design documentation (schematic diagrams, etc.) to this European organization. After reviewing the schematic diagrams against the samples, it was discovered that the submitted documentation was different from the samples. Electronic components' values were intentionally changed to hamper success. When confronted, the Far East lead design engineer admitted that the design documentation was intentionally changed prior to sending it to Europe. There was a severe urgency to get an improved design completed and to supply a more robust product to consumers. Valuable time and money was lost due to this.

Subsequent conversations with the Far East head engineer indicated that he was not going to give his team's hard work away to another organization. There is a problem in Chinese cultures with intellectual property theft and they thought that they were protecting it. During many conversations, I was unable to convince him that we were all on the same team and cooperation was the only way that the organization would be able to get acceptable product to its consumers. Many heated conversations did not result in me getting through to him, he still maintained that the correct thing was done.

In this part of the world, Intellectual Property (IP) theft is common. This is something that has been in the Chinese culture for thousands of years and I believe that the engineer and my client were victims of this.

Subsequently, the engineer was forced out of the company. Enhanced product was eventually produced but severe damage in the market ensued, resulting in poor sales. This organization struggled to stay in business.

Cultural issues can be destructive if one allows them to be.

4. An Uprising on a Ferry

Here is an example of when a situation escalated in a fashion that I was not used to seeing.

Once, while on a ferry going from Hong Kong to mainland China, I witnessed an interesting situation.

As I was boarding the ferry, along with a Hong Kong associate, there was a large Hong Kong Chinese group embarking at the same time. As expected, this group of Hong Kong Chinese conducted themselves very orderly and docile. During the seating, there was a quiet discussion with one of the ferry employees that lingered for a while. This is what I expected to see. Suddenly, as if a bomb went off, it accelerated into a loud and disorderly shouting match. Many individuals were simultaneously shouting in Cantonese and the situation became out of control. My experience is that the Hong Kong Chinese are very reserved and polite. I have never seen this type of behavior in Hong Kong before.

I asked my Hong Kong associate to tell me what was going on, as the shouting was not in English. She said that there was a disagreement relative to the seating arrangements. Further questioning revealed that this culture is normally reserved and polite, however when a threshold is broken, things can go from calm to bedlam. There is no gradual acceleration of tempers.

I learned something new about the Hong Kong Chinese culture on that day.

5. Habla con el jefe (Speak with the Boss)

A valuable lesson relative to getting a commitment

At an event that a client was hosting, I became engaged in conversation with an employee of that client. He began to complain that he was getting what he thought was a firm commitment from a business contact in South America. During multiple conversations, he received assurances that the there was agreement for an action and that the task would be accomplished quickly. However, nothing happened and the person that I was speaking with did not understand why.

I inquired as to the level in the organization of his contact and if that person had the authority to commit to whatever was needed. He insisted that he did, as his contact was part of the corresponding department. I immediately took issue with this and recommended that he speak with the head of the department and not a worker. He disagreed with me and indicated that it was unnecessary. Eventually, he did take my advice, spoke with the boss and obtained results.

In some developing countries, there is still a very autocratic management style in organizations. Workers, even professionals, are not delegated the authority to make decisions and they will not admit it. The boss, and only the boss makes decisions. This is what happened here.

It is wise to try to assess a sense of the management style in place and *habla con el jefe,* if in doubt. *You are not in Kansas anymore.*

6. The day that the lights went out in China

A wasted trip to a facility there

While performing supplier work at a facility at an Asian country (not China), I had to schedule a visit, along with my client, to their factory in China. We requested that this visit be performed on the following Friday and the supplier agreed. We flew to Hong Kong the day before and met the supplier, as scheduled, just over the Mainland China border. Upon entering the factory, we noticed that the lights were off and the building was empty. The government had imposed a forced *blackout*. This part of southern China suffered from a shortage of electricity and each factory needed to be shut down one day per week so that the available power could be rationed. Friday was the day for this factory to be shut down, so there was no activity for us to witness and evaluate.

As a condition of awarding this business, the factory needed to operate 24/7. When asked how they planned to comply with the work schedule due to the blackout, the supplier produced a purchase order for some diesel generators. Our schedules did not permit us to return on an alternate time. Subsequently, I was unable to determine if this was the best fit for my client and they were not awarded the business.

This resulted in wasted time, travel expenses and futile efforts, which I believe were caused by cultural factors.

Their cultural norms dictate that in China one does not say no nor push back to those in authority. They will sometimes avoid saying no or delivering a negative message. In this case, we were not warned that the factory would not be operating so as either of us would not *lose face (mianzi)*.

Upon returning to Hong Kong that evening, I came across an interesting article in the newspaper. The forced blackout caused many factories in the Pearl River Delta Region to order diesel generators so that they could meet their delivery commitments. The one local factory making these generators was very busy. One day the government knocked on the generator factory door and informed them that they were required to shut down one day per week. This factory did not even think of keeping a few of their generators on hand so that they could maintain operations for the entire week. It seems funny that an organization that manufactures electric generators could not operate because of a lack of electricity. I believe that the next few generators to come off the line were kept by them.

Beware of cultural issues, as they can be devastating.

7. No deliveries for Christmas, $5 Million down the drain

Arrogance and lack of cultural understanding caused these individuals to lose their jobs

While assisting an assembly plant in Asia, I witnessed a cultural error that cost a company to lose $4 Million US in sales and lose some high-ranking personnel. This company was managed by Westerners. The plant assembled consumer products where a very high percentage of the items were sold worldwide at Christmas time. Most of the components were sourced in China. These Chinese component suppliers had long established lead times for orders that my client honored in the past. Past deliveries were mostly made on time.

While planning for the Christmas rush one year, the assembly facility management decided that the suppliers did not need the established lead times and placed the orders late. No attempt was made to negotiate shorter lead times with these suppliers. There was an arrogant attitude something like: *they are our suppliers and they must comply with whatever lead time we give them, we are the customer and they must serve us.* Component orders were placed and there was no push back from these suppliers, just silence. *In this case no news was not good news.* My client concluded that there was no problem and that deliveries would be made as requested. This proved to be a big mistake as the Chinese culture was not considered. In this culture, the lack of a response can mean that a problem exists.

Consequently, the orders were not filled on time and the assembly facility could not produce enough product to fill most of the customer orders. This resulted in lost sales (~$5 Million), retail space given to competitors and considerable customer dissatisfaction. Some retail space was not recovered during the following years. The two top management personnel at this assembly facility were subsequently forced out of the organization.

The Chinese typically do not push back to anyone who they think is in a position of authority. Due to a possible *loss of face* and other cultural considerations, silence ensues rather than delivering a no answer or a message that is negative. This is what happened. Rather than tell their customer that they could not deliver and negotiate an alternative, the suppliers remained silent. The management concluded that *no news is good news. This was a big time c*ross cultural miscommunication error.

The assembly facility also failed to consider cultural differences and did not realize that no response spells trouble. This company ended the fiscal year at a loss and two executives lost their jobs. I have seen many similar situations that could have been avoided with cultural savvy. My clients need this skill and it is why I began to conduct cross cultural training / coaching. This training is vital to success.

On another note, the company also spent $5 Million on educating these two managers and then got rid of them.

Some individuals feel that retaining them and using this expensive education might have been a better option.

Arrogance and lack of cultural consideration has no place in the successful business world.

8. The One-Child Policy

This is what happens when one does not stay away from certain political / sensitive topics in the presence of foreigners.

At a meeting in Malaysia with client representatives from various world locations in attendance, I witnessed a young American engineer make a cultural *faux-pas*. This was back when the Chinese one-child policy still existed. It has since been modified.

There was a Chinese person, who lived in Shanghai, at the meeting. In front of a group of us, an American engineer asked the Chinese individual what he thought about the one-child policy. The answer he received was that it is the law and it must be followed. Not pleased with the response, the American insisted and kept asking the same question. He continued to get the same answer. I finally motioned to him to stop with this inquisition as it was not going anywhere. His insistence was making us all uneasy and the Chinese individual was not going to share his opinion, as he was probably afraid to do so.

I did privately explain to the American engineer that in countries with an autocratic form of government citizens are careful not to express feelings which are contrary to government policies.

Freedom of speech does not exist everywhere in the world and speaking against the government or their policies can have negative consequences (sometimes even prison time). In international settings, political and other controversial subjects should be avoided.

One should exercise care when broaching topics of discussion when in international settings. Stay with safe topics such as sports, art, literature, history, personal interests, travel and the weather.

9. Doing it for the wrong reason

I learned a valuable cultural lesson.

During one of my first encounters in China, I attempted to help an organization. Initially, I was not successful.

While working with this supplier, who performed machining of components, I saw a need for them to try out a system that would most likely help them produce compliant parts. This organization was having difficulty making these within the required dimensional tolerance. Some of the parts were being made to the incorrect size.

I wanted them to try a charting technique (pre-control charting) to see if this would help. I spent time explaining to the person in charge of production the theory behind this and instructed him, in English, on how to proceed. He was provided with some paper forms to use at first. My supplier contact was Hong Kong Chinese and was fluent in English. Just to make sure I had my associate explain it to him again in Cantonese, his mother language. It was stressed that it was a tool that would help him and that I would return in a couple of months to follow up. If this proved successful, we would then help him to implement this formally using an off the shelf computer generated system.

Upon our return, he proudly showed me the completed forms and said: "we filled out these papers for you". I asked him if he interpreted the results and used the results to understand and improve the process, he displayed a puzzled look. It became obvious that he did not attempt to use this information, he was just looking to please me.

I did not realize back then that in this culture, sometimes, blind obedience to any authority is expected. I had not spent enough time stressing that this was an improvement tool for them to use and not a form to be completed for submission to a customer.

This was one of my faux pas.

Part II

ON THE LIGHTER SIDE – AMUSING EXPERIENCES

10. "... but I don't know how to drive"

In some regions, the rules are: there are no rules.

I spent about seven years traveling to an assembly facility located in Southeast Asia, where I became very familiar with the players. This was a very rewarding experience as I was successful at implementing multiple operational excellence projects, which resulted in cost savings and quality improvements. The culture there was very open to the implementation of improvement tools / approaches and the professionals there were eager to learn. My need to develop organizations and individuals was satisfied there.

One day I needed to visit a local supplier and asked the facility quality manager to accompany me. He suggested that I go with the young engineer who was responsible for this supplier, instead. I agreed.

This is one of the few Asian countries where I was brave enough to drive in, so we departed in a company car with me driving. Upon finishing up at the supplier I offered to take the young engineer to a nice lunch at a local shopping mall. On our way, we encountered heavy traffic and I was in a bit of a rush as I needed to be at a meeting right after lunch. I decided to make an illegal left turn. As luck has it, there were two policemen right there and I was stopped. They advised me of my infraction and asked to see my driver's license. I normally lock up my passport, return air ticket, US currency and wallet in the hotel safe. I carry with me is some local currency, a photocopy of my passport and an international driver's permit. This time, I had forgotten to bring the driver's permit with me. I explained this to the policemen and offered them the documents that I had with me. They then said that I needed to accompany them to the police station. I tried to talk my way out of the situation to no avail. The young engineer then offered to supply his license and have them issue the ticket to him instead. They agreed and began writing the ticket. I asked the engineer how much the fine would be. It was the equivalent of ~$5 US, I proceeded to take out the money to give it to the engineer. The policemen then began to eye the money and, at that point, it became obvious to me what they wanted. I suggested that I give them the money so they could pay the fine for me; they agreed and proceeded to tear up the ticket. Then, the police and the young engineer switched from English to the local language and the young engineer became visibly nervous. Finally, after an emotional exchange we were permitted to continue. I then asked the young engineer what happened. He indicated that because I did not have my driver's permit with me they wanted him to drive. I said: "so why did you resist driving, I do not care if you drive." He said: "I don't know how to drive, I bought my driver's license."

I also realized that I bribed two policemen for $5.

Just because someone has a driver's license, does not mean that they can operate a car.

11. Do not play games with interpretation

A manufacturer in New Jersey made a costly assumption relative to language comprehension of a potential customer representative.

My first consulting client was a large US multinational corporation. I was engaged for 9 months to perform supply chain improvement work for them. Their main production facility was suffering from multiple supplier issues resulting in constant production interruptions. They needed these resolved.

While working at one of their suppliers in the northeastern US, I received a call to quickly wrap up what I was doing and travel to this potential supplier in the area. My task was to perform a quick evaluation on this facility and report if I thought that they were worthwhile. I reluctantly followed this request and arrived at this prospective supplier late in the afternoon.

Upon arrival, my contact indicated that the person running production did not speak English well and that he needed to interpret for us. I speak some Spanish and usually begin my interaction in Spanish, when appropriate, to help with establishing rapport. I did not do it this time and it worked out for the better.

I asked questions in English and, at first, did not pay attention to the interpretation. Eventually, I realized that my contact was asking the foreman unrelated personal questions and then telling me what he wanted me to hear. I was getting a real *snow job*. I allowed this to continue and began to practice, in my head, what I would say in Spanish upon leaving. I wanted it to sound perfect and shock them. Upon leaving, I thanked him for his time and said that I would report my conclusions to my client, **all in what I believe was perfect Spanish**. His reaction was shock and his jaw may still be on the ground sixteen years later. Subsequently, I recommended that my client not walk away from this organization but run.

It is not good practice to assume a lack of language skills.

12. Eating Breakfast with Adam Sandler

By mistake, I got to eat with this famous actor

I was engaged to perform some supply chain training and speak at a conference for a professional organization in South Africa. After two long flights and a three-hour ride to the hotel in Sun City, a bellman proceeded to escort me to my room. He pointed to where I should go for breakfast the following morning. I also heard that a US studio would be shooting some scenes for a movie at this hotel over the next few days.

The next day, I proceeded to where the bellman had indicated that I should go. It appeared to be configured as a movie set. I attempted to enter the dining room and was stopped by someone with a badge that indicated *set director*. He asked me if he could help me and I indicated that I was looking for the breakfast. He directed me to another area. When I arrived, I was stopped and asked if I could be helped. I indicated that the set director told me to come here, so I was allowed in. Before long, I realized that this was the private breakfast for the cast and crew of the movie *Blended*. I helped myself to my morning meal and stood next to Adam Sandler, who was joking with another cast member. Soon, the cast was called to the set and I left with the group, still walking next to Adam Sandler.

My intent was not to force my way in, it just happened.

13. No scrambled eggs for me in China that day

This frozen cook just could not do it.

During a stay at a newly built hotel in northern China during the dead of winter, I was not able to eat scrambled eggs for breakfast even though they were on the menu.

Heated buildings are not that common in China. It is normal for employees who work indoors, in both offices and factories, to wear coats, hats, gloves and scarves while at work. Upon checking in to this newly opened hotel, I noticed that there was no heat in the lobby; however, my room did have heat. The next morning, I went to the hotel restaurant to have breakfast and discovered that this area was also not heated. This was the newest and best hotel there. I had to go back to my room to fetch my coat. I did not want to shiver while eating.

Upon my return to the restaurant, I went to the egg station to order some scrambled eggs. The poor person working there did not have a coat on and was obviously freezing. I placed my order and he then proceeded to prepare the eggs. After breaking the eggs and placing them in a bowl, he attempted to scramble them with chopsticks. He was shaking so much from the cold that the eggs were falling out of the bowl. He could not keep from shaking long enough to keep the eggs in the bowl. After three attempts, I had to settle for eggs over easy. The yokes broke because he could not hold the spatula steady, but I ate them anyway. Otherwise, I would have needed to wait until spring to get what I wanted.

Dress warm if you go to China in the winter. There may not be heat.

14. Do fire extinguishers really need to work?

To this day, I am not sure why this factory did not know the obvious.

A western organization asked me to perform a pre-review of a facility in China. My client was very interested in awarding them some business and asked me to help this organization pass the upcoming new supplier audit. I needed to detect problem areas and give them guidance on how to rectify potential problems in advance of the audit to ensure that they received an acceptable audit rating.

One of the items noticed during the assessment of this newly built and empty building, was the absence of fire extinguishers. My host indicated that there was no plan to install any fire extinguishers. I then told the Managing Director that he needed these to pass the audit. He was provided with the number of fire extinguishers needed, how to install them and the required spacing. He agreed to obtain these and install them correctly.

Some weeks after this visit I passed by this factory on my way back to the ferry dock for my final transport to Hong Kong. Most Chinese factories in the Pearl River Delta look the same, however this one was somewhat unique so I recognized it. I was with a Hong Kong Chinese associate who served as my guide/translator/interpreter. I indicated that we needed to stop in and check on the status of the problem areas that were detected during our last visit. My associate indicated that we could not visit without providing them with advanced notice. My answer was B...S.... I told him to tell the driver to drop me off and that I would go in alone and find my way back to the ferry dock. He did not need to accompany me. I was going in with or without him. Reluctantly, he came along. The guard at the facility gate announced us and the Managing Director came running out very excited and surprised that we did not provide him with notice of our visit. We said that we were early for our ferry and were passing by. I just wanted to make sure that everything was OK for the audit.

The Managing Director very proudly showed me the fire extinguishers that he had purchased and installed. They had gages installed, which showed that the canisters were empty. I picked one up, tapped it and verified that it was empty. The others were empty as well. We asked him what he planned to do about this and he indicated that he thought they were fine like that.

Fighting to control myself, I informed him that these were useless unless they were charged. He seemed surprised.

I am still not sure if the cause of this was ignorance or a way to save money.

15. Left-handed chopsticks

This is when I demonstrated that this westerner had better chopstick skills than some Chinese.

I mastered the use of chopsticks early in my travels to China. I like to eat and there were many restaurants there that did not have forks, so this skill was a necessity for me. It took me some time to learn the use of these implements but I did.

The Chinese like to watch foreigners struggle with chopsticks as they find it amusing. Once at a restaurant in China, one of my hosts watched me carefully, was impressed and said: "you have good skill with chopstick". I thanked him for the compliment. He then asked me if I could pick up a peanut with chopsticks and I did it. The entire group was very impressed. I boasted that I could even pick up a peanut left-handed. I had never tried this before but just got lucky and succeeded. It was a bit of a miracle; I could never do it again. I then asked the other Chinese to see if they could pick up a peanut left-handed. They all tried and none of them could do it. As they struggled, peanuts began to fly all over the restaurant. At one point one of these projectiles hit me. I was the only one to do it left-handed. I then accused them of being fake Chinese and me being the only genuine Chinese in the group. Never again did I try that stunt again.

Maybe this is the reason why I was given the Chinese name *Ho Man Kai* by some Hong Kong business owners.

16. Soup on a Plane

My wish finally came true on this flight.

I had always wanted my wife to spend some time with me in Asia. After many years of asking her to come to Asia, I finally got her to agree. She flew to Shanghai to meet me and the plan was for her to spend a week there. We had friends living there as expats that she could spend time with.

During her visit, my client redeployed me to Taiwan and we needed to depart mid-week. During this time, due to political reasons, there were no direct flights to/from Mainland China and Taiwan. We needed to take a Chinese airline to Hong Kong and then transfer to a Taiwan-bound flight.

My wife has much better table manners than I do. The manners that I possess are based upon my environment growing up in a working-class neighborhood in Brooklyn, NY. My parents did not finish high school and never knew enough to teach me proper table manners, thus my many *rough edges*. My more sophisticated wife is refined at the table and is usually critical of me. I warned her that it is normal for the Chinese to make noises while eating and to expect it. In spite of the warning, I knew that she would not like it anyway. I was hoping she would experience it and I would be amused at her reaction. I had been waiting to experience her reaction for a long time.

On the plane ride from Shanghai to Hong Kong, I hit the jackpot. She was in the middle seat with a Chinese person on one side of her next to the window. I was in the aisle seat. Soup was served as part of the meal. *Hot soup on an airplane that is subject to turbulence? I could not believe it.* Her seat mate commenced to slurp his soup providing her with a concert of various noises. I had fun watching her nonverbal reactions. She was visibly having a very difficult time. I had to hold in my laughter.

Upon departing the aircraft, I asked her how she enjoyed the concert during our lunch. She indicated that it was a very disturbing experience, to say the least.

I got my wish and then some!

17. These stairs are a challenge

The most unusual staircase I have ever seen.

Most factories and assembly facilities constructed during the recent Chinese economic expansion are mostly similar, simple but functional, and somewhat safe. This time I found myself in one that was not.

While climbing a flight of stairs in an old assembly plant in China, I detected that something was wrong with my ability to climb them. My legs were acting funny; they felt like they were giving out. Surprisingly, there was a handrail present that I could hold on to; many other older facilities did not have them in that region. I needed to grab the hand rail to avoid falling. I thought to myself that if I needed medical attention I was going to insist to be brought to a hospital in Hong Kong and not mainland China. Upon looking back at the staircase more carefully, it became obvious to me that the height of each step was different. It seemed that no two steps were the same height. Nothing was wrong with my legs. The problem was with the inconsistent step heights. With that in mind, negotiating the steps was not much of a problem. I just needed to move more slowly and be more careful than usual.

More of a concern is that in the event of an emergency evacuation, such as a fire, the workers rushing down the stairs could potentially be falling over each other.

18. Why does he care?

I have seen many poor safety practices throughout the world, however, this one "takes the cake".

During an assessment of an assembly facility in China, I noticed a foul chemical smell in an area used for processing product. This caused me to *follow my nose* to the source. I witnessed some workers using a chemical, which turned out to be the source of the odor. The containers were labeled in English something like: "do not breathe vapors or allow to come in contact with skin." The workers were not wearing gloves, there was no exhaust hood to remove the harmful vapors nor were the workers wearing any respiratory devices. The chemical was all over the workers' hands and they were directly breathing the vapors. I asked my interpreter to ask one of the workers if they understood the safety warning on the containers. The worker answered that she did not understand English and had no idea as to what was written on it. I confronted the manager accompanying me (who spoke English) about this situation, stating that he may be killing his workers. He then said something to my interpreter in Cantonese. For cultural reasons, I decided not to ask for an interpretation. Shortly after that incident, the tour was completed and we departed for Hong Kong.

On the way back, I asked for the translation of the remark that the manager had made earlier. The interpreter said that the assembly plant manager did not understand why I cared about the workers. Like many other organizations in these regions, they had a lack of concern for their employees.

Even though things have been getting better in this part of the world, situations like this still occur. We, in the west, need to continue to push for reform.

Part III

INTERESTING FACILITIES – TO SAY THE LEAST

19. The fire at a supplier in Latin America that killed a product for my client

I hate it when a client does not want to listen.

I was performing a productivity enhancement (LEAN) project for a supplier to a Fortune 100 US multinational organization. They had a major supplier of finished product located in Latin America. This supplier produced all product for the Americas.

I have been doing facility assessments since 1972 and cannot help but notice many problematic situations. Safety violations, among other items, seem to just jump out at me. I feel obligated to report these observations to clients even if they are not the reason for me being there.

On the first day at this Latin American facility, I noticed that some of the overhead sprinkler heads (used for automatic fire suppression) were missing. I suspected that the system was not operational. The management of this facility admitted that they had problems with this system and had shut it off the year before. Notwithstanding my recommendation to repair the system, they indicated that there was no plan to make repairs. I reported this situation to my client, as it was an unnecessary risk that should be corrected. The cost to mitigate this risk was small and there was no reason not to make repairs. When I informed my client, he was annoyed, indicated that I should just do what I was sent down there to do and not to bother with other items. He did not want to know about this and did nothing to pressure the supplier to resolve this potentially risky situation. The supplier ignored my second plea and did not repair the system. Making these repairs is cheap insurance, as the consequences could be and were, indeed, severe.

My project was successfully completed. The supplier was then able to produce enough product and costs were reduced. Both the supplier and my client were delighted with the results.

About a month later, I learned that a large fire had ensued at this factory and it was no longer able to produce product for my client. Immediately, I called the client and they engaged me to help with the assessment, recovery and refurbishment of the production tooling located in the burnt-out rubble. I also performed the qualification and production at alternate suppliers in Asia so that the product flow could begin again. Critical time was lost and customers began canceling orders because they did not want to wait for product. My client lost significant retail space and market share for that product. This lost market share was never recovered. I still have difficulty finding this product on retail shelves. In addition to the lost sales, the recovery effort resulted in a high cost to my client. They needed to pay me, take engineering talent off other development projects to work this effort and pay startup costs to three other suppliers in three separate countries in Asia. A functional sprinkler system could have prevented this. The cost of the needed repairs was relatively inexpensive.

In addition to the effect on my client, the supplier could not recover from the fire and went out of business.

It is not wise to ignore safety items and other risks with your operations and supplier management system. I am happy to see that the new version of the international standard ISO 9001:2015 (Quality Management System) requires registered companies to address, analyze and mitigate risks. Hopefully, this will save some other companies.

20. The employees were eating lunch on the dirty floor

This is an example of an organization setting themselves up for a disaster.

I was asked to evaluate an assembly facility, located in an Asian country, for a European client. The company imported kits and performed final assembly at this plant. This allowed them to lower their import duties.

There were many complaints and unresolved disagreements between the assembly facility and the kit supplier located in China. This situation resulted in assembly difficulties, poor consumer performance, numerous complaints and higher than expected product returns. They were losing money.

One of the complaints was that the paint finish contained imperfections. I did not even need to enter the assembly facility to discover the problem source. Upon driving into the assembly facility grounds, I noticed that product was being stored outside, under trees. I thought that these were old or scrapped units and was told that they were finished product ready to be shipped. There were birds in these trees that were defecating on the product waiting to be shipped. This was causing the paint imperfections. I did not even enter the building and there was a recommendation that the finished product be covered, if stored outside. At that point, I realized that I was in for an unpleasant (and memorable) experience. I just looked up at the sky and thought to myself: *here we go again!*

We then passed by an outside storage bin containing a sign *SCRAP*. Some parts were being unpackaged and placed there. When asked of the status, I was told that these were good parts that were just delivered from the supplier. The danger here is that when the recycling company came to pick up scrap materials the good product would be inadvertently thrown away. That is why, in a well-run facility, good and bad parts are to be separated and controlled. This also prevents the inadvertent use of defective parts /assemblies. This was the second major issue discovered before I even entered the building.

Upon entering the general assembly area, I noticed workers sitting on the very dirty floor sorting hardware (nuts, bolts and washers). This hardware was just dumped on the floor and then placed in the appropriate container. There were no available tables for this operation. In looking at some samples, I noticed that there was dirt in the threads with no plans to clean them before use. This caused difficulty during assembly and possible loosening / disengagement during consumer use. Some could even result in a consumer being injured.

One operator was observed striking a component containing a polished finish, which he was having difficulty assembling. He was using a steel hammer, thus causing cosmetic damage that a consumer would see. This part was supposed to fit into the mating component easily; the appropriate action would be to investigate and correct the cause, not hammer the part in. If it needed to be forced in, using a soft mallet, rather than a steel hammer, would have been a better method.

Part of the assembly process involved the use of an assembly line with a conveyor. In one case, I witnessed an operator stop work to answer his mobile phone. While he was talking on his phone, the product was going by without him installing the part that he was responsible for. I am not sure whether some finished product left without all the necessary components.

A foreman came over to me with a tire inner tube, which had punctures. He stated that the inner tubes shipped by the supplier were defective. Upon further inspection, it was obvious to me that these punctures were not a manufacturing defect but were caused during the assembly process. I then asked to go to the tire assembly area. The operator was installing the inner tubes into the wheel assembly and inflating the tire. I asked to see a tire and wiped my fingers inside and found much grit and dirt. It is accepted practice to blow or vacuum out the dirt prior to assembling the wheel. As the inflated tube was being pressed against the dirt in the tire by the air pressure, the dirt/grit/debris caused the punctures. The assembly facility caused the punctures, not the inner tube manufacturer.

Painted components were stored on the bare and dirty floor without any protection. Damage to the finish ensued and the supplier was being blamed.

It was lunch time and I saw the workers eating their lunch while sitting on the very dirty floor. The management did not provide tables and chairs for the workers to eat at. I thought I had seen everything, but this one was new to me.

The paperwork (production travelers) was not being completed properly. There were many missing entries. I was unable to determine if any assembly steps were being skipped. My suspicion is that some critical operations were not completed and some product departed the facility incomplete.

It was darker in the final inspection and acceptance area than the balance of the assembly area. When asked why, I was told that they wanted to save on electricity so some lights were turned off. It seems that providing inspectors enough light to find defects was not a priority. I had seen this before as it is common in this part of the world.

They were blaming most of their problems on the Chinese supplier of the kits; however, it became obvious to me that the assembly facility was the cause of many of the above concerns. The Chinese kit supplier owner was asked to visit this facility to show her the defective parts. I strongly recommended that this visit be postponed until they got their *ship in order.* My fear was that she would see some of the poor practices and not accept their claims. As expected, they did not take my advice. She did visit, saw these items and refused most of the claims.

Unfortunately, this move backfired for my client. I did not want to be right this time but I was.

This division eventually went out of business.

One should take the time to engage the right supplier and not buy on price alone. Consider the total cost.

21. Paying to make a bad situation worse

Here is an example of an improvement project gone bad

A very large multinational US based organization contracted me to perform an operational excellence (Six Sigma) project. They needed to improve a very time-consuming and defect-ridden data system. It was common knowledge within this organization that the resultant data summaries were inaccurate and management was unable to make sound business decisions based upon this system.

My main client contacts were trained in Six Sigma and I thought that they knew how we should proceed and the pitfalls of not applying this process correctly. They impressed me with their knowledge of the improvement tools but their overall approach was far off. Subsequently, I was forced to proceed in the incorrect manner.

This process works when the actual workers are engaged in analyzing and improving a process. The workers doing the job every day know the actual process and know how to improve it. They are the true experts, not supervision nor management. Experience has shown that a team of 6-10 members works best. The tools used are powerful when used properly. I have worked with many other organizations who have reaped significant benefits and cost savings using this system. This approach works well and produces significant positive results only when employed correctly.

Things did not start off well. In the early afternoon of my first day on site, I was told that I did not have the appropriate authorization to be there. I needed to depart the facility immediately. Assurances were given that I would be able to come back the following day and that I should just stay in my hotel room until called in. This was neither a government nor military facility and a security clearance was not required. I do not know what clearance was needed and I spent the next four days captive in my hotel room waiting for a call to come in. I would rather work fifteen-hour days than be idle like this. The client paid me for my time and expenses, with no output.

The client put together a team of about twenty-five, high-level management personnel from around the world. These individuals were not the ones who performed the work and were not the true experts on how to improve it. It was impossible for them to define, analyze and improve a process they did not understand. The other problem was that the size of the team was well beyond optimum. It has been proven that problem-solving teams this size just do not work. Another issue was that each time we met, some team members changed making it difficult to move forward effectively.

The project proceeded with the assistance of another consultant. I then had a death in the family and needed to leave the project for some time. Upon taking care of family matters, I decided to not continue with this project as the other consultant was enough to finish it up. The client agreed. I suspect that my personal value system kicked in and would not allow me to continue to take money from a client where they would get no benefit.

I later learned that the client did not improve nor simplify the process but, instead, made it worse. They added complexity, which resulted in increasing the amount of inaccurate data. With the consulting fees and international travel of the client's team members (First Class plane tickets from Europe and Asia are not cheap), this probably cost this client about $ 1 Million. All to make a bad situation worse.

There is a saying in Spanish for this. They went from Guatemala to guatepeor (from bad to worse) and spent significant money to do so.

22. Most product is reworked

Reworked / repaired assemblies are never as good as ones newly assembled.

Back in my early days as a consultant, I was asked to evaluate an electronics assembly facility in Asia. The organization I was representing was considering them as a supplier.

While touring the assembly area I was rushed passed a room with a closed door. The small window was covered. My experience in evaluating numerous such facilities told me to investigate, as this is usually something being hidden and it must be seen. Immediately, I stopped dead in my tracks. Upon questioning the person conducting the tour, he said that I did not need to see that area. That caused me to dig in and insist that I was not moving until he took me in there. I indicated that the other option was that the tour would end immediately and I would recommend that this organization not be approved. With this threat, we entered the room. This room was used for rework of failed product. There were more workers doing rework than building new product. To this day, I have not seen another assembly facility with more rework personnel than personnel producing new product. Components were being unsoldered from failed circuit boards. There were piles of components, circuit boards, displays, etc. on the floor. The manager indicated that they just re-use most items without any re-testing. Some of the components were mostly not functional and they were just reusing them. Multiple studies have demonstrated that reworked electronic assemblies are less reliable than virgin ones. The extra unsoldering and handling damages these components.

This facility was experiencing a high in-house failure rate and the quality level of shipped product was questionable.

Fortunately, my negative recommendation was accepted and this supplier was not used.

Beware of assembly houses like this, as they exist all over the world.

23. Are suppliers the enemy?

Suppliers are supposed to be business partners but not for this organization.

One of my first consulting engagements was with a major US corporation located in the USA, which purchased packaging from suppliers. The bulk product manufacturing and filling of these packages was performed at their own facility. I was brought on to resolve the many quality issues that they were experiencing with the purchased packaging. These issues kept causing the factory to shut down production lines causing missed shipments and increased costs.

This organization was a good example of what not to do relative to managing suppliers. They treated suppliers as the enemy and not business partners. A significant number of incoming product rejections were due to this client and not the supplier. It was almost as if my client purposely wanted rejections, so that they could extract financial concessions from suppliers. When I could demonstrate that the supplier was not at fault, some individuals within the client's organization expressed displeasure with me. The answer that I received was "now we cannot charge back the supplier". This factory looked to blame their failures on suppliers and not look inward so that their processes could be improved. This tended to cover up problems and imbed them into the organization. They suffered many avoidable production shutdowns due to this behavior. This added costs and caused production delays. I wish that I had the opportunity to analyze this further and substantiate this avoidable waste. The significant financial loss would have opened their eyes and maybe changed things for the better. I have always wanted to do the right thing at the expense of being unpopular but, this time, I was not permitted to. My frustration mounted.

This attitude permeated within the organization. I found myself in the middle of constant disagreements between suppliers and my client. There was evidence that the suppliers charged my client extra for this *grief. The one in the middle of a p...ing contest is the one that gets wet,* as they say. After about nine months, I decided to not serve this impossible client and did not renew my contract. They lost money the year before I was with them and for some years after. It is a wonder that they are still in business. My suspicion is that their continued survival is due to the rather large margins for most of their products.

Suppliers are business partners and are an extension of the organization that they are serving. A good company wants their suppliers to be successful. Developing suppliers and fostering productive relationships are paramount for success. Organizations that have an active supplier development program receive enhanced performance from their partners. My many years developing suppliers have taught me that they are not the enemy and should not be treated as such.

24. My most frustrating experience as a consultant

This place almost killed me.

I was engaged to perform a production launch of a new consumer product for a large USA based multinational corporation. The product was designed in the USA and my client subcontracted production with an Asian (not Chinese) organization. The factory was in China but not owned nor operated by Chinese. I spent five weeks on site in China, working seven long days a week. The original plan was for me to be there for just two weeks. By the third day I knew that I was in for a longer stay. I missed Thanksgiving with my family that year (no turkey for me that November).

The product being manufactured needed a clean environment; however, an actual *clean room* level was not required. Prior to entering the production area, I was given clean replacement footwear, a lab coat and a hat. After dressing, I entered an air shower which is intended to blow off surface dirt. I was initially impressed by this level of cleanliness as this was more than necessary for the product being manufactured there. The site manager first entered the air shower and used it incorrectly. He just stood still. The correct use of an air shower involves raising one's arms and rotating so that most of the dirt/dust is blown off. I should not have needed to inform him of this and soon began to become unimpressed without even entering the production area.

Once inside, I noticed that the rear door was open. There was a building under construction adjacent to this one and a lot of airborne dirt/dust was entering this room. Employees were entering through this open door and tracking in much dirt and mud. This area was extremely dirty and contained an unacceptable environment for the manufacturing of my client's product. I thought to myself: *here we go again,* as I have seen many other facilities like this in the past and knew what I was in for. It took me three days to get them to keep the rear door closed and force the employees to enter through the air shower. The entire room needed to be cleaned before I allowed the production of first samples. In a very short time, I became disheartened. Here are some situations that I dealt with:

> The production manager was the only person available to me who spoke English and served as my interpreter / translator. Being that the management style was very autocratic there, he was constantly getting phone calls from the factory floor. There were times when it took me over two hours to get an answer to a quick question due to all the phone call interruptions. If his mobile phone did not ring it was the office phone. Sometimes both phones rang. This severely slowed my progress and was a major factor in this product being launched late.
>
> The production manager was newly hired and unfamiliar with the company and technology. He did not have sufficient authority, needed to ask

permission from the home country office for routine items and was insecure. This also hampered progress.

The necessary support and test equipment was either nonexistent, not available or not working. One measuring device needed a special light bulb and it took them four weeks to procure one. Another needed test device was available; however, no one in the facility was trained on how to use it. I was constantly sending samples to my client in the USA for testing or measurement. It took four days to get results that should have been available on the same day, had the needed equipment been available for use.

There were multiple quality assurance tasks that needed to be accomplished prior to production approval. I needed to interface with the one quality manager who covered all the multiple (about twelve) production buildings. One Monday, I was informed that he was with another customer and would not be available to me until the following week. At this point, I thought that I would never get to go home.

Some critical measurements needed to be recorded and statistical calculations made. I convinced them to purchase a Chinese version of the needed software. The software is written so that the operator making the measurements can enter the measurement directly into the computer. As what was typical in China at that time, the management did not allow production workers to use a computer (I guess that they were afraid that the production workers would break the mouse) so they entered the data on a paper form and then office workers needed to reenter the data into the computer file. It has been proven that reentering data results in errors. It took one week for me to get the results and the accuracy of the results were suspect. There were some obvious gross errors.

They were using an automatic raw material mixing device connected to the production machine which I knew was another company's design. The engineering department of this organization admitted that they stole the design, reversed engineered it and illegally manufactured a copy. When asked about how they tested (calibrated) it to ensure its accuracy, I was told that this was not performed and they were not sure if it was accurate. They just slapped it together and began to use it. I could not accept that the raw material ratio was correct so a sample was provided for my evaluation. There was supposed to be no more that 6% of one item in the mixture. My personal testing indicated that it was in fact 16%. Another issue that held up progress was that my client needed to perform more testing to ensure that this mixture was compliant to regulatory requirements.

Some other raw material needed to be processed in another building and I asked to see the area and witness the mixing. By then, it became difficult for me to believe anything that I was told and was compelled to verify most things. My job was to protect my client and I always took this responsibility seriously. I was first denied access to this building. It took three days of conversations among all three parties to finally grant me access. The area was very dirty, not clean enough for this material and its final use. I also noticed an overhead, leaky pipe. Soon, I realized that it was a waste water pipe. The raw material was being contaminated and a few drops of this waste water fell on my head. Of course, the first thing that I did upon returning to my hotel was to shower and get that sewage off me.

One day I was ready to go to lunch and was asked for permission to start one machine. The table where finished product was to be placed was dirty and I indicated that it needed to be cleaned first. The manager then told a worker to clean the table. I returned to this area about three hours later and witnessed the same worker still cleaning the table. He was told to clean it and was apparently not allowed to stop until someone told him so.

Fortunately, he did not wear a hole in the table nor his hand.

There were not enough storage bins available to meet the production needs. This was discussed on the first day of my visit. I was assured that this was not a concern, as more bins could be made or purchased quickly. The supply of bins soon ran out and dirty cardboard boxes needed to be used instead. Five weeks later, upon my departure, the new plastic bins were still not in place.

Some parts, under warranty, from one production machine failed and the manufacturer of the machine needed to provide replacements. These badly needed parts remained in Chinese customs an extra four days due to a dispute over who was going to pay the customs duty. I was told that this was less than $40 US. This amount seems minor when compared to its urgency. *The supplier should have paid the duty and resolved this with the manufacturer later. Four critical days were lost over less than $40.*

The factory did not have direct phone lines out of the country; they needed to use prepaid phone cards. These cards kept running out during critical phone calls to my client in the USA. We sometimes could not complete the call until the next day due to the unavailability of another prepaid card.

They did not have a dedicated speaker phone for the building that I was in. There was one to be shared with three different buildings. Often, a conference call to my client was not possible due to the lack of a telephone.

The facility did not have a fax machine and when asked to have something printed or copied the wait time would be two days. I had someone take me to Walmart where I bought them a copier-printer-fax machine for ~$60 US. Subsequently, I was informed that the owner was embarrassed because I needed to buy them this basic device. My answer was: *he should be.*

I asked for two file folders to organize some papers. They told me that they did not have any to give me as they were too expensive (at no more that 5 cents each). *Interesting way to treat a customer that just gave you an $8 million purchase order.*

I needed to deny permission to begin making product on a newly-configured machine, as there were dead insects all over it. They really thought that it was ok to run the machine in that condition, notwithstanding the fact that the product needed to be sanitary.

They did not have enough resources to support my client's production. On many occasions, I detected intentional delivery delays of production tooling done to cover up this situation.

Towards the end of my stay I detected poor inventory control process. To help ensure that they would not run out of raw materials, I had them store the raw material in the production area, in full view, rather than the warehouse. It would be visually obvious when stock got low. They complied with this request. I asked them to insert a visual marker at a location where new material would need to be ordered as double insurance. About three weeks after I left, my client contact called me and said *s... of a b...., those! @#!@# ran out of raw material and production is shut down for six days!* I just shook my head.

These five weeks were spent at an inland city in China, so far west that it seemed that most residents had never seen a westerner. I was a spectacle, when in public. People were even bringing their children to see me.

I was staying in the best hotel the city had to offer, marketed as 5-star lodging. The bathroom's tub enclosure was covered with mold. I had to buy bleach and attempted to clean it myself; even scrubbing the grout with straight bleach and a toothbrush did not get rid of all the mold. I felt as if I was showering in a giant petri dish.

Whenever I needed to leave the hotel for shopping or to go to a restaurant I asked the bellman to tell the taxi driver where I needed to go. When I am in non-English speaking countries I always carry the hotel business card, which contains the address, with me. Sometimes it took me up to five different drivers to find a literate driver who could read the address in Chinese characters and take me back to my hotel.

The one good personal result of this experience is that I used some of the money made on this engagement to have a sun room installed over what used to be my deck. I enjoy this during the warmer months; however, it still reminds of what I went through to get it.

If I did not live this one, I would not have believed it.

25. There were many positive outcomes, it was not all bad.

In reading the past chapters one would conclude that these problem facilities were the rule. They were the exceptions.

I have experienced many well-run manufacturing related organizations in China, Taiwan, Malaysia, Thailand, India, The Philippines, Hong Kong, Puerto Rico, Dominican Republic, Mexico, France, Germany and the USA. My consulting involvement with numerous projects in these regions resulted in operational improvements, increased quality levels and cost savings. These successes provided me with much satisfaction and a sense of accomplishment.

One example was when I conducted two LEAN projects in a large maintenance facility in Southeast Asia. This client needed significant cost savings to remain competitive. I was selected as their consultant, over some stiff competition, for this project because of my experience with the local culture. Processes were analyzed by the actual workers using a powerful tool - process mapping. Group problem solving / improvement tools were then utilized by this team, with me as the facilitator. The commitment to this client was for a $6 million annual savings and my personal goal was $8 million. A conservative estimate at the end of these two projects came in at a $11 million annual savings. This organization had a very competent management team. They provided the necessary support and involvement to me and the employee teams. This is a vital element for success. The

CEO was the best one that I have come across in my 45-year career.

Another $4 million success happened almost by mistake. I was assisting a US client in implementing a Quality Management System (QMS) so that they could achieve registration to ISO 9001 (the International Standard for Quality Management Systems). One of the expectations of this international specification is that the organization understands the interaction of their various processes. During process mapping exercises with the various departments I noticed that the purchasing and material organizations both performed stock level assessments upon receipt of sales orders. This wasteful duplication of effort caused me to investigate this more. Subsequently, I discovered that there was duplicate ordering of expensive raw materials by both departments. It was also noted the stock room was larger than the production floor. This was due to an over inventory of this expensive raw material. When this was brought to the attention of management, I was immediately redeployed to this new task of resolving this situation. After a rather short period, the duplicate inventory assessments were eliminated, thus saving wasted labor. The inventory levels were adjusted to meet production needs and eliminated unnecessary money being tied up in inventory. The stockroom size was reduced and the added room was converted to production. This eliminated the need to lease another building. The annual savings enjoyed was $4 Million. Over the course of the following year, I received multiple communications from the purchasing manager thanking me for saving her about six hours a week.

A client in Latin America was experiencing difficulty in meeting the production volume needs of one of its customers. The one semi-automatic machine was unable to be run at maximum speed due to the operators' inability to load and unload product fast enough. I was engaged to reduce the manual loading and unloading time so that the machine would run at maximum speed. The production speed was increased through engaging the operators, analysis and video recording of the faster operators. Product began to flow to the customer at the expected rate.

There were many more; these are just some examples.

I have seen a gradual improvement in the management and performance of these types of organizations through the efforts of western corporations, eagerness of these organizations to learn better manufacturing / assembly methods and government support.

26. Conclusion

I have had the good fortune to travel around the world and see it not as a tourist but as a businessman. These extended times on the ground, interfacing with locals provided me with insight into how individuals in other regions think, act, communicate, live and view foreigners. This opened my mind and provided me with significant personal growth: however, it came at a price. There are no free lunches in life, the price that I paid was the time spent away from home.

Hopefully, this book allowed me to share these experiences with those not performing this type of work and provided those involved with similar work some valuable lessons.

Here are some parting recommendations:

> Prior to working with individuals from another region, take the time to learn their culture. As a minimum, perform some research on the internet or read a book on world business culture (there are many out there). Even better, attend a training session or bring in a competent trainer to your workplace. Hopefully, the section on "It is not right or wrong, good or bad, it is just different" drove that message home. This small investment will posture you for success and may help to avert a disaster.

In spite of the fact that offshoring / outsourcing is slowing, there are still opportunities for businesses to take advantage of lower labor costs and to sell in other countries. I strongly recommend that you do not enter any type of business relationship until a competent professional performs a thorough evaluation of the operation that you are considering. Make sure that all the hidden costs are addressed and secure a detailed agreement relative to the required resources. Look carefully before you leap and avoid the disasters described in chapters 19 and 23. Avoid being infatuated by a low price, consider the total cost.

Lastly, consider the following fourteen tips that I created as guidance during the early days of my consulting career:

Ho Man Kai's fourteen tips for implementing improvement into Chinese organizations:

1. Realize that you are compressing 40-50 years of growth and change in the Western World into 1-2 years in Chinese organizations, a formidable challenge.
2. Research, understand and apply the Chinese culture. This will work wonders.
3. Become actively involved in the improvement process. The Chinese expect this.
4. Select on-site support personnel wisely. Technical competence is not the only factor.

Other qualities and skills can be more important.
5. Encourage and assist your Chinese partners in supplier development activities.
6. Tailor the application of improvement techniques to fit the Chinese culture.
7. Understand that the word "no" is considered hostile/disrespectful. Do not expect to hear it.
8. Realize that "yes" may not mean agreement. It may mean that the message was heard and nothing more.
9. Perform a comprehensive evaluation of facilities and systems with a Westerner who is experienced in working with and developing Chinese Organizations.
10. Realize that ISO 9001 registration may not mean that the organization has an acceptable Quality Management system. Perform your own survey.
11. Actively become a part of the process when selecting local training. Engage someone with actual application experience. Proficient and experienced personnel may be hard to find in China.
12. Work towards retaining the key Chinese personnel that you have developed. Understand and address their cultural, social and developmental needs.

13. Encourage your Chinese counterparts to ask questions and challenge you. This will take some effort and skill.
14. Learn and apply "Mianzi" and "Guanxi".

www.ingramcontent.com/pod-product-compliance
Lightning Source LLC
Chambersburg PA
CBHW070318230526
45470CB00002B/934